CODEPENDENCY

How To Detect Toxic Relationships, Discover Narcissistic Personalities, Regain Control of Your Life and Stop Being Dependent On Others

By Daniel Cloud

© **Copyright 2020 by Daniel Cloud - All rights reserved.**

This document aims to provide accurate and reliable information about the topic and issue covered. This publication is sold with the understanding that the publisher is not required to render any qualified services such as accounting, officially permitted, or otherwise. A practiced individual in the profession should be sought, if professional advice is required.

Table of Contents

Introduction 6

Chapter I: The nature of codependency 10

Chapter II: Signs of codependency. Do you recognize yourself? 26

Chapter III: Self-esteem and how we think about ourselves 42

Chapter IV: Strategies for an increased self-esteem 56

Chapter V: Jealousy: why do we feel it? 76

Chapter VI: How to manage jealousy in relationships 88

Chapter VII: Codependency: How to say, "Stop!" 100

Conclusion 109

Introduction

Relationships are a fundamental part of our life, and there is no doubt about this evidence. However, it seems like we are living in a time where we have become increasingly aware of how vital these personal interactions are to us. From having a partner who we can spend our life with to having friends who will support us no matter what, relationships are necessary because human beings are social beings in nature.

In addition, relationships teach us many important values and lessons about others, and ourselves so this also means that without these interactions, we would probably have a lot of trouble trying to decipher the world that surrounds us.

Relationships also make us more grounded and compassionate; they make us stay in touch with each other's needs, and they make us feel empathy with -and towards- the community we live in and the individuals that belong to it.

However, it is also true that relationships can be tough to nurture and to maintain, especially if our self-esteem and self-worth are not congruent with how we see and present ourselves to others.

However, in reality, this can all be a farce as well, because you may be dependent on another person without needing to acknowledge it, which requires you to work on yourself. This is because, when an individual suffers from codependency, he or she also tends to show other symptoms that go hand in hand with this dependency characteristic.

However, and just to give you an idea, if you are having problems with your self-esteem, then you may also be in a codependent relationship. On the other hand, you may have problems whenever you trust another person even if you are overly dependent on them. You may also be a jealous person because deep down, you don't trust the other person in your relationship.

You may be scared of being hurt, and this is why you are codependent on another person because it not only makes you feel better, but you have also found your *"safe place"* or your *"safe person"* even if you would never admit it to yourself.

On the other hand, if your partner is codependent on you, then he or she may also have low self-esteem. They may show jealousy signs, and they may not know how to get out of this dark place where it seems like all of their energy is going into waste by thinking negatively.

However, if you genuinely want to change, then you must understand that this transformation will require a lot of effort and patience on your behalf as these changes will not occur overnight.

In fact, you will work hard on yourself and be diligent with how, what, and why you are feeling a certain way. You will also need to be open-minded, especially if you are living and experiencing old and destructive habits and ways of being that you have installed deep down yourself.

This isn't an easy process and it can even take years to understand it. And, on top of this, you will have to let go of your old ways so you can move on peacefully with your life purpose because the most important relationship you have at the moment (and from now onwards) is with yourself.

Thus, this means that you will first need to heal to then heal your relationships with others.

It can also happen that during your healing process or soon afterward, you start to realize that those relationships you thought were good are everything but that.

You may also understand that the biggest mistake we all make when we are in a relationship is to want the other person to be how we want them to be instead of how they indeed are.

And once we see our mistakes with an open heart then we realize it's sometimes too late to do anything about it. But we can always change now and become a better person in the future.

If you would like to know more, then I'm here to tell you that there are many ways in which you can change this codependency and have your life back.

You can become a person who lives a truly independent life where you honor yourself, where you stop being in a codependent relationship with others, and where you start enjoying your life and your decisions again because your self-esteem is high. You do not depend on others to regulate your mood.

By listening to this audio book you will be given with simple but very efficient strategies to overcome jealousy in your relationships, increase your self-esteem, and stop being codependent on another person.

Chapter I: The nature of codependency

Are you in a relationship that requires a lot of effort on your behalf? Do you have a friendship that always makes you question how and why you are doing some things or how you are reacting to situations, even if you previously were decisive about them?. Do you unwillingly spend all of your energy on those people? Or perhaps you sometimes feel like you are the one who's always making sacrifices for the other person?.

And, lastly, aren't you tired of feeling like this?, Isn't it exhausting to be always thinking about the other person and their needs and desires, instead of focusing on yourself and what you want and need, right here right now?

If you are always giving up on those things that you want and if you don't see the problem in this attitude, then you may be in a codependent relationship and this can cause you to live an unhealthy lifestyle with long-term negative consequences. But the worst part of this is that you are not really aware or conscious about either of these things.

Where does the term Codependency originate?

Codependency is a psychological concept that has been around for years now and explains the dependence of a person on substances (could be either drugs, alcohol, or both). According to psychologists, a person in a relationship can also be called codependent because they will have the same characteristics and traits of a dependent person, regardless of the dependency they have.

However, do you know what a codependent relationship is? What does it entail? Is it something that cannot be changed, or do you have the power to see this as an opportunity to rise above these issues and gracefully move on?.

Because if you want to get your life back and if you would like to understand how you got to this place in the very beginning, then you must understand the meaning of Codependency in terms of relationships.

Codependency and relationships

A codependent relationship is when a person (either you or your partner) are in a constant need of approval from each other. Thus this behavior becomes a fixed pattern in your life because thanks to that approval you always seek, you will then validate yourself, your worth, and your life.

In other words, in a codependent relationship, a partner needs the other partner. And, on the other hand, there is a partner who needs to be needed. Thus he or she becomes the enabler because they enable this situation to continue. In addition, this non-stop need, in turn, forms a circular relationship where there is constant codependency on the other individual. Then the cycle of a codependent relationship has begun, and for some people, this may be difficult to stop.

Codependency Vs. Dependency

However, what are the differences -if any- between a codependent relationship and a dependent relationship? Aren't these types of relationships the same as individuals are still dependent on another person?.

This is a fundamental question and it can lead you to understand the differences that exist between a healthy dependence on another person and a codependency trait, which can be very harmful.

Here is how I illustrate these differences in terms of relationships. It doesn't matter who this relationship is with, as long as two (or more) people are involved.

- Dependence: If two people are in a relationship, then they will both support and love each other equally. This means that both of them will have important values and roles within this relationship, and neither of them would ever doubt them.

Codependency: There is always one individual in the relationship who either feels worthless or doesn't know their position within the life of their partner unless the other person explicitly says it. On the other hand, the enabler takes advantage of this and enjoys being the center of attention of the other person.

- Dependence: Even though both parties are happy with each other and they spend a significant amount of time together, they are also aware of the importance of taking care of their other friendships as they are all necessary to nurture in order to maintain a healthy lifestyle, so they make time to see them.

Codependency: There is a lack of values in one of the individuals in the relationship because they simply cannot see how much they are worth. There is no need to have a personal identity because they think they have everything they need within their codependent relationship. Thus they don't have problems if they never get to see any of their old friends again. In fact, once a person is in a codependent relationship, they will likely leave all of their friends behind.

- Dependence: In a relationship, both individuals are allowed (and encouraged) to express themselves and to overcome issues and problems together. This not only means that they will feel closer and more in sync than ever before (as they were able to solve something together), but it also means that they will both benefit from choices that will strengthen their journey as a couple.

Codependency: In a codependent relationship, one person feels the need to express their feelings, whereas the other person feels like it's almost a waste of time and energy to do so. Usually, this individual has a tough time trying to recognize what, how, and why they feel the way, they do. So, of course, it's entirely normal for them to have a hard time when communicating to others what's inside their minds and hearts.

- Dependence: An individual who is in this type of relationship is not afraid to experiment something new. This could be that they take on a new hobby or they learn some crafts. They are always looking into ways of improving themselves because this makes them happy and at peace.

Codependent: A codependent person is sometimes even afraid to leave the house. They find comfort in staying in their homes, especially when they know that there is a big world out there.

Who can be codependent?

Codependency can affect everybody, as it doesn't make a distinction on race, gender, cultural backgrounds, or political sentiments. So, if you are a spouse, a friend, a coworker, a sibling, or a parent, then codependency can be affecting you or those who surround you.

Therefore, codependent relationships don't have to be romantic relationships only. In fact, they can be between friends, family members, and even work colleagues, so wherever there are human beings and a society then codependency can exist.

Repetition occurs in individuals who are codependent

Also, when a person is dependent on one relationship, then they can find themselves being codependent on another relationship as they tend to repeat emotions.

For example, Julia is in a romantic relationship with Alex. She is in love with him, but she's also very codependent on him. He is aware of this too.

Julia is timid, and this has led her to feel uncomfortable at work as well, so she relies on her coworker, Patricia, to speak to her managers on behalf of her, because she can't do so herself. So, whenever Julia has a problem at work, she goes to Patricia instead of talking directly to her boss.

Therefore, codependency can lead individuals to have a dysfunctional relationship where one person will rely on another person to meet his or her own needs.

Being codependent can also mean that other areas in one's life can suffer. From having problems with a professional career to having issues trying to do everyday chores, being codependent can be seen as if a person is carrying a burden.

Continuing with the previous example, Alex, who is the enabler of Julia, his partner, is, in turn, codependent on another person: his mother. Alex's mom knows that his son relies on her and is codependent on her. She also knows that he wouldn't dare to make up his mind about something without asking her first. So, Alex's mom takes advantage of this and makes her son act and react however she pleases.

The codependency cycle continues

In a relationship, either person can become codependent on the other person, or it is a common mistake to think otherwise. Once this occurs, then they will feel unequal, more than ever before, and this can take them to a challenging and dark place.

Usually, the codependent individual will forget about their emotional and physical needs, and their self-esteem will now be at an all-time low. Also, their focus will remain on the emotions and the self-esteem of the other person instead of looking within themselves to see how their emotions are self-esteem are.

And this can lead to severe problems as both individuals in that relationship can feel exhausted, anxious, stressed out, and even depressed. This type of relationship where codependency is encouraged can also lead to a promotion of dysfunctional behavior where they prohibit and prevent each other from learning essential life lessons that are necessary in order to thrive in today's world.

In some cases, this type of relationship can also include emotional, physical, or spiritual abuse, and even though this may seem weird or odd to outsiders, the reality is that the couple won't see it for themselves. In fact, they will disagree with others if they are trying to warn them that they are engaging in a complicated and unhealthy way with each other.

Being codependent means that your sense of purpose in life will be valued by the sacrifices you make that will, in turn, satisfy your partner's needs instead of your needs. It also means that an individual will be encouraged (even if it's done silently) to continue with their irresponsible and addictive behavior that will perpetually feed the codependent relationship.

It can be argued that a person who is codependent on their partner, will plan their entire life around them, and their partners will be more than happy to see this because they will want to receive their other half's sacrifices as a way of showing their true love.

Every day codependency

These sacrifices can be anything; for example, your partner got promoted to a better paying job, but you would have to move to a different city or country. You weren't too sure about this massive transition and change, yet again, you decided to agree because you wanted your relationship to work.

A couple of months have gone by, and you are now settled in this new place. However, you are not happy at all. You don't have any friends or family members around, you don't speak the new language, and your partner is always working.

And what's the worst part about all of this? You have genuinely tried to fit in. You have taken language classes, you have gone to free activities to get to know different people, and you have come to terms with the fact that your partner will spend a lot of time working away.

The reality is that you don't like this new place, and you cannot wait to get out of there. However, you will not dare to tell yourself (nor your partner) this. What's more, you end up staying there living and feeling miserable because deep down, you know that this isn't the best place for you. But how can you say that to your partner and crush their dreams, especially considering they only just got their dream job?.

Does this sound fair to you? Does this sound healthy to you?.

Another example would be: you are a grown-up woman who works hard, and you recently got a one-off bonus, so you are now deciding whether to buy an apartment or a small house. You call your mum to tell her this and she "advises" you to get a car because, by doing this, she can get a ride from you to go to her medical appointments.

You really wanted to get the house, but now you are considering getting a car because your mum is right, she's getting older now and, eventually, she will need your help, and if you get a vehicle then this will solve all of *her* problems. So, what do you do then? You get a car, of course!.

Are you able to see the common point in these two examples?

You are letting go of those things you truly wanted so the other person can be happy. In the first example, you are willing to live a life you dislike just because your partner received an excellent job opportunity. In the second example, you are willing to change your mind entirely and get something you hadn't even considered before because you want to please another person.

In both examples, you are willing to exchange your inner peace, your desires, and your well-being for feelings of stress, tension, anger, and even confusion, as you slowly become aware that what you are doing is not something that you wanted to do. Instead, you decided that someone should take the lead of your life and determine what's best for you.

It's like you depend on someone else to be happy. And this codependency can affect all of us at some point or another because absolutely anyone can become codependent.

Whenever you give up on your own needs or even your identity in order to meet someone else's needs, then you are starting to display signs of an unhealthy relationship, and this can cause severe damage both on your short-term life and in the end as well.

Is there a way to change a codependent relationship?

In a balanced state of mind, everyday clinginess doesn't necessarily equal codependence as there's no more to this than the simple and basic need of being next to someone and being able to feel them close to you, so, you could argue it's not even clinginess anyways, it's only the need of having physical contact.

Contrary to the above, being codependent is far more extreme than being clingy because when you are in a codependent relationship, then neither you or your partner are aware of it.

Being clingy is not necessarily a good thing either, as this habit can become very unhealthy, especially when traits such as self-sufficiency and autonomy have decreased; however, it cannot be compared to codependency.

The development of Codependency

How does a codependent relationship begin in the first place?. Is it something biological and innate to us, or is it something we learn from others?

When we are born, and all through our childhood, we are incredibly dependent on our caregivers. Because of our size and our lack of skills, we are vulnerable to the outside world as soon as we leave our mother's womb and start facing the real world.

We need our caregivers to provide food, safety, comfort, and love 24/7. In fact, we also need them to regulate these things for us, as we are only able to sleep, do our basic needs, and feed ourselves. From our births on, we are intrinsically dependent on others who will, in turn, help us survive.

This is why it's so crucial for new parents to talk to their child, as this will also guarantee a bond with them, a relationship that goes beyond any physical contact. Still, it's so unique that it can also create an immediate attachment.

Once we start growing up, we also begin to explore our independence. We start crawling, walking, eating solids, we walk, we run, we jump, we are continuously learning from the environment we are in as we are fully exposed to it.

So, it is only logical that if you grow up with a parent who had to give you all of their attention, love, and affection, then you will try to replicate this later on in life, because it will also make you feel safe, loved, and comfortable.

On the contrary, if you grew up with a parent who was often unavailable or unreliable, then you will grow up thinking that this situation was and is healthy, and all parents are like this.

Therefore, you will believe that it is okay for you to put your parents and your partner's needs first, as this is what was done to you for so many years.

In other words, once we all grow up and become adults, we start repeating the same familiar dynamic that we were involved with when we were younger.

Dysfunctional families and codependency

Another relevant characteristic of a dysfunctional family is that they don't have the need to talk about how their dynamics are, and they will try to avoid this subject as best as they can because they feel extremely uncomfortable when trying to address these issues.

So, codependency can be seen as a "give" and "take" operation, when on one side you have an individual who will act as the caregiver role (which is also referred to as the enabler). This person will immediately say "*yes*" to the unasked question of *"would you take care of me and others?"*.

Then on the other side, you have another individual who loves to receive as much attention as possible. These two types of people will eventually form a symbiotic dynamic where they too will fall into the habit of codependency.

Innate or learned behavior?

Many psychologists argued that codependency is a learned behavior because, at some point in your life, you witnessed someone who had these behaviors, and now you are a grown-up, you are copying them.

For example, codependency was directly linked to alcoholism and drug addiction, so experts used to think that being codependent was a result of living with one or two parents who would display these problems, therefore, it became a learned behavior.

Why are you codependent on another person?

Researches show that there are many possible reasons behind a person who becomes codependent on another person.

- Overall negative parental relationships

Research has shown that if you, as an adult, have problems being codependent, then it's likely that your parents were also like this.

You probably grew up in a very conflicted household where addictions were the norm. Perhaps one of your parents was an alcoholic or drug user, either way; you saw firsthand how those who supposedly had to take care of you, would put their own needs first.

You probably learned the hard way that your needs weren't as important as your parent's needs, and somewhere down this line, you could have started thinking that your needs weren't important at all. So, you didn't learn to validate how you feel, because no one took the time to teach you how to do it in the first place either.

Sometimes, when parents are needy, they even teach their children that they are selfish or greedy if they start communicating what they want to say, think, and or feel.

It almost feels like these children are not allowed to thrive nor to experience anything by themselves. And, as a result of these constrictions, the child will learn to ignore their feelings, and they will think that what the others feel is way more important than what's going on inside of them.

In addition, in a situation like this, the child will be deeply affected, as their integrity and emotional well-being are deeply compromised. An individual whose childhood was complicated is prone to have a problematic emotional development because they didn't have positive examples to look up to when they are growing up. Therefore, it is very likely that they will end up being in a codependent relationship as well.

- You live with a mentally or physically ill family member

Having a physical or mental disease is complicated, and there is no doubt about it. If you have lived with a person who has continuously suffered (for instance, someone who is chronically ill), you may have witnessed this despair and suffering for a long time.

Codependency can also be a result of this situation, especially if during your childhood or teenage years, you were the caregiver of this person. Maybe you naively helped this other individual without receiving anything in return.

You then developed your personality, and helping others is something you are proud of and, above all, you enjoy doing it. And there's nothing wrong with this either, except when it starts affecting your life and the way you see yourself.

Anyway, do not forget there is always an exception to the rule, as living under these circumstances does not mean that you will end up being codependent. However, it does mean that in environments like these, it is more likely to have, show, and install dysfunctional behaviors such as the ones listed previously.

Going down the line

What's more, because codependency is a learned behavior, this can be passed down from one generation to the next.

Thus, this will continuously affect all individuals who behave this way, as they will not be able to have emotional and healthy relationships that can be satisfying to all parts.

It can be known as a "relationship addiction" because, as the name suggests, you can become addicted to being in a relationship. You will spend a lifetime going from one relationship to the next because you will feel like your relationship is lacking something, or you are involved in a destructive relationship pattern.

However, an individual can overcome codependency in many ways. Because, ultimately, even if we are social beings and we love to take care of others, especially those important people in our lives who we genuinely love, everybody should be responsible for their own lives, mistakes, and good deeds.

You are not, and you should not feel responsible for what your parents did when all of you were younger. And it is now up to you to take a look at yourself and see codependency for what it really is: which is a stone inside your shoe that doesn't allow you to walk correctly.

What will you do then? Will you walk uncomfortably for the rest of your life and complain about every single detail? Or will you take the shoe off, take that rock out and throw it far away from you?.

This is definitely up to you. You cannot change your past, but you can definitely improve your future now.

Chapter II: Signs of codependency. Do you recognize yourself?

In the previous chapter, we analyzed the nature of the codependency and you should now be aware that being codependent is a psychological condition that is often paired with a mental or emotional health issue.

You now also know that everybody can go through codependency in their lives, especially if they have come from a dysfunctional family where physical, emotional, and or sexual abuse were, unfortunately, a reality.

When an individual has been abused or has experienced traumas in their life, then he or she has grown up and molded themselves with some dysfunctional personality traits that will lead them to become codependent on another person whenever they are in a relationship.

Therefore, many people will automatically act in the same old way without thinking they have another choice. In addition, every time they try to get into a new relationship, they will be repeating the well-known broken patterns they had experienced when growing up because he or she continues to think that this is the only reality they know.

As a result, people will not have clear boundaries in their relationships. They will not know who they are nor who their partners are (they genuinely think they have become one), and they will continue to live and breathe a dysfunctional relationship.

This lack of boundaries leads us to the following point: try to think about the unhappiest couple you know. Once you have that couple in your mind, then try to think about the reasons why they are still together. Do they have kids? Are their finances bad? Do they fear going their separate ways even if their relationship is unhealthy? Or do they stay together because they are both dysfunctional in their own and unique ways? They are either blinded by the situation they find themselves in, or do they choose to ignore it?.

Because, unbelievably, people do stay together -even if they are miserable- because they think that the other person *needs* to be with them or to have them by their side.

And what's worse is the fact that they might even have the best intentions and they truly would love to feel and experience love in a healthy way, but they do not know how to do this, and they don't think they need help either.

However, a combination of their experiences, their ignorance about how to turn this over, and their actual behavior will make them doubt themselves like never before, and this is great when it happens as it means that there is room for improvement.

And even though they will probably end up asking the vital question: *"why?".* So, *"why is this happening to me again?" "Why do I have to go through this?" "why can't I be loved and give love the way I truly deserve?".*

They will still be able to understand why and how they are codependent and, if they have started their path towards healing, then they will change the question of *"why?"* And will turn it into a *"what's next?", "What do I do from now on?"*

Then, reality hits, and depending on the person, they will come face to face with two options or scenarios. In essence, they can go back to the old destructive patterns of codependency in their relationships, or they can try to comprehend what is going on and try to overcome these issues consciously.

A brief reminder about codependency

It's important to understand that a codependent individual is often trying to excuse themselves into thinking that someone else needs them.

This person will now start feeling useful because he or she will need to take care and nurture the other partner, even if that person is continuously engaging in unhealthy behavior that can be damaging (such as being an alcoholic).

Then, resentments will start appearing as both individuals cannot even recognize their own needs anymore. It seems like they don't have control over their lives. Therefore, they cannot direct themselves in any way because they don't know where to go.

Signs of codependency

Nowadays, you can find a lot of statistics, scientific research, and even questionnaires about this topic. So, how do you know if you are in a codependent relationship?

If you and or your partner are showing any of these signs, then you must re-evaluate this relationship as it might be codependent and, therefore, unhealthy.

Remember that this is just a simple guide, so you will also need to use your discernment.

- Do you often feel lonely even if you are with someone else? You may be spending time with a specific person, but you still feel alone, as if nobody can understand you.

- Are you starting to see unhealthy reactions and behaviors in your partner (or yourself), but you remain in a said relationship despite them?. Because you either feel comfortable being in this relationship or because you are scared of going on your own.

- Do you often support others despite risking your own mental, emotional, and physical health?. It's like everybody's needs will come first, and if you have time at the end of the day, you will think about yourself for a couple of minutes.

- Has your partner or any significant other people in your life have ever told you that you are very dependent on them?. It could be your son or daughter or your co-worker. Maybe they see things you have not seen before.

- Do you often feel anxious? Especially when you are in a relationship?. Like you cannot get yourself together, and you are often thinking about the future instead of focusing on the present.

- Do you spend a lot of time thinking about how you'll be happier once your partner changes certain conducts or characteristics of their behavior?. Because you cannot see how you should also change something if they don't commit themselves to do it differently as well.

These are all real questions, and you should be telling yourself real answers as well. It's difficult, I know, life and relationships are equally tricky, but you shouldn't feel like you can't handle either.

In fact, the answers you have given yourself will make you feel stronger, even if you don't see this right away. Because once you start organizing your thoughts, your problems will also move the underlying energy they hold, and things will become more evident if you let them.

And what if you negatively answered these questions? Do not worry! These signs of codependency can turn into something better by the end of this guide.

So, if those were some signs, what are the symptoms of codependency?.

Codependency and its symptoms

This is a list of traits, patterns, and habits that codependent people have in their codependent relationships.

As you will see, there are many different symptoms, but you don't need to have them all to qualify as a codependent person.

- People pleasing: If you are a codependent person, then you will not stop until the other person's needs have been met.

It's challenging for you to say "no" to something, especially if that special someone in your life asked you to do something.

Of course, it's fine to want to please others, but if this causes you anxiety or negative feelings, then you shouldn't be thinking about pleasing another person. Instead, you should focus on pleasing yourself.

You must acknowledge this, so next time someone asks you to do something you don't feel like, then ask yourself this: *"what will I gain if I do this? Will I be okay, or will it cause me anxiety?.* If the answer is "okay" then go ahead, you are following your lead. However, if the answer is anxiety, then run away! Listen to yourself!.

- Low self-esteem: if you are a codependent person, then your self-esteem is likely to be low, unfortunately. You may start thinking that you are not good enough, pretty enough, smart enough.

You will continuously compare to others who you think are better, prettier, and smarter than you.

You may feel unloved or misunderstood by others, but the reality is that you feel this way because you don't love yourself enough, and because you don't understand your processes.

- You feel as "controller": if you are a codependent person, then you may also feel like you need to have absolutely everything under control to be happy.

There's no way your life can have unexpected situations because you become too anxious and do not know how to respond to them.

In fact, having everyone and everything under control means that you have done your job well, and you can now feel safe. If you are codependent, then you wouldn't like living in constant uncertainty, chaos, and confrontations because you know you will not be able to have your say on those things.

- You cannot communicate effectively: If you are a codependent person, then you may have problems when trying to communicate to others how you feel, what you think, and what you need.

It can also happen that you don't even know how you feel, and this can cause problems too. You may feel like lying or "omitting the truth" because you are afraid you will hurt someone's feelings.

So, you may not like something, but you won't say anything about it because the other person likes it. Then whenever you are communicating, you are dishonest because you are not speaking your truth.

- You are dependent: if you are a codependent person, then you rely on another individual. It seems obvious, doesn't it?. But to some people, it's not.

You are afraid of being neglected, rejected, and or abandoned, thus you overly clingy to a person to try to avoid this. You cannot stand being alone.

And whenever you do end up being with yourself, you will quickly find a new relationship to go into (even if it means that you might end up being abused again), or you start feeling depressed and anxious about your new loneliness.

It's like you are feeling trapped inside your body, and the only reason to escape from your mind is if you are with someone else.

- You react instead of respond: if you are a codependent person, chances are you don't think about responding to a situation, but you innately respond to the situation.

Did someone say something about your culinary skills being terrible? How dare them! Do you not agree with what a person is saying? How dare them!.

The lack of boundaries also means there's a lack of understanding of others. And, as a result, absolutely everything and everyone will find a way to get to you, and you will end up becoming defensive.

- If you are a codependent person, then you may have problems whenever you are trying to understand what your feelings are and how you can feel them in order to overcome them.

Codependency can create stress, anxiety, and even painful emotions such as fear of being judged, fear of not being loved, fear of being alone.

You may also be scared of making mistakes, being a failure, feeling trapped within your body, you may be resentful, angered, hopeless, and you may end up living depressed and in despair.

However, if you feel like you are ticking all of those imaginary boxes and you see in yourself all the codependent symptoms, then try to relax as these should only be taken and considered as an informational guide.

How does a codependent person behave?

Usually, codependent people have low self-esteem in comparison to independent people. They also tend to look for an external cue to make them feel better and to validate how they feel.

More often than not, codependent people will find it hard to be themselves; thus, they are not open to meet new people or to go out to new places.

This is when they start trying additions and or addictive behaviors that, if left untreated, can cause severe problems to them.

And even though they have good intentions, they will still be misunderstood because *"how can they come to be martyrs if another person is also suffering?"*.

There is no doubt that when these destructive episodes kick in again, they will swipe everything that is on the surface area. Thus, you must be prepared, and you must know that if you want to quit this habit, an old way of thinking, then you are not and will not be alone.

Can a codependent person recover from this?

There is hope - and help - for codependent individuals who would like to live a healthier and happier life.

The first step a codependent person should take is to get in touch with a specialist who will offer him or her professional guidance and support.

Being in a codependency relationship means that you have probably witnessed quite a few tricky things in your life, and perhaps not many other people would be able to handle this at all.

This is why counseling and or therapy are highly encouraged as they will provide you with the necessary tools that will help you become more assertive and more in tune with yourself.

Codependency and a new opportunity in life

Because of all the symptoms mentioned above, codependency will require you to see a specialist who can help you and guide you in order to overcome this issue and succeed in both your personal life and working life.

If you are a codependent person and you are wondering about the things you could do now to become more independent in your relationship and become a healthier pair, then you are already on the right path.

Because as soon as you find out that you or the one next to you is codependent, then there's no need to break up the bond you share immediately, thinking that this is the only or the best solution you could come up with and work towards it.

Of course, if you feel like breaking up is the option, then go for it. But sometimes relationships need a little guide that will save them, especially if the individuals are meant to be with each other.

This is why a therapist would bring an excellent insight into how things are going in your relationship. In fact, and if you truly wanted it, you could both repair your relationship together, alongside your therapist.

But how do you do this? Especially when, in some cases, your trust may be broken.

First, you will have to repair your self-esteem. You will need to understand that perhaps you did things because you didn't know better. You will need to stop judging yourself and or seeing yourself as a victim, so the other person can stop judging you and painting the "victim card" at you.

Secondly, you could set some healthy boundaries. So instead of completely shutting off, you will be focusing on yourself now; whether people like it or not, it doesn't affect you anymore.

It's also important to see your friends and family and spend time with them. You could also find a new hobby to do or become more active by doing some exercise.

You can also start feeling resentful because you are leaving old patterns behind and don't recognize your own needs anymore. This is all part of the process, and you should live this as well so you can come out stronger from the other side.

Scientific research has found that these symptoms are reversible, so if you don't treat them, they will only get worse and will continue to damage your life even more.

This psychological treatment will often involve an in-depth look and search for your childhood. And as you navigate these waters, you will probably see how much you have copied from your parents as a defense mechanism and how much you continued to act like them, making way for the dysfunctional behavior patterns to rise.

Once you are in therapy, you will also be encouraged to explore the moments when you started to feel disappointed, hurt, angry, and needed. By doing this, you will be able to see how this has shaped your relationship dynamics.

Being on the right track

You will know when you are finally on the right track because you will feel better, you will sleep better, and your overall well-being will be at a new time high.

You will also start to adopt new personality traits for your new life:

For example, you will consciously nurture yourself. You will put your needs first, and you will decide with whom you would like to bring in to have a connection with your inner world.

In addition to this, you will see yourself under a new light, where you are now capable of understanding how smart, pretty, reliant, and intelligent you are.

What about the codependent relationships you had? Well, if the other person has worked individually as well (as in they have assisted therapy, and they have become aware of their own self-destructive patterns) and if they are ready to work as a couple, then why not? Of course, this may be complex to solve, but it's not impossible.

If, on the other hand, you decide to stay single (but never lonely anymore because you are with yourself!) Then it is excellent news as well! You have now said goodbye to abusive behavior that isn't needed anymore.

You are now able to respond instead of reacting and attacking the rest of the world. You realized that once you changed your perspective of things, things will also improve their perspective of you.

And, lastly, you can tolerate external opinions, but you are also able to disagree with them without getting too involved. You adopt a conscious way of living where you are aware of your thoughts, your actions, and of course, your reactions.

What happens next?

If you have started working on yourself, you have been attending therapy sessions, you have become aware of your emotional, physical, and mental health, and you are now turning your life upside down, then it's only a matter of time before you ask yourself this question.

What happens next?, What is the next chapter of this adventure that we often call life?.

When you are on your path of recovery from codependency, then you will no longer feel the need to satisfy another person but yourself. And this isn't an egotistical thing to do or to say, quite the opposite. You deserve to feel this, especially after all the time you spent taking care of others and forgetting about the most important person in your life: you!.

Once you are on your way to recovering yourself, you will not feel the need to be in a painful relationship. You'll be able to smell a destructive relationship from miles away, and you will be comfortable whenever you need to turn around and set up a new direction for your life.

But what happens if you feel ready to be in a relationship? It could be with a new person or with an old flame if both of you have worked thoroughly on your issues.

More specifically, how do healthy relationships work?

- People who have come out of a codependent relationship should take small steps whenever they are adventuring into a new relationship.

In order to make this new relationship work, they will need to stay in touch with their family and friends regularly. It would also be useful to participate in new activities or consider new hobbies.

We all know how great it is to spend time with a person we are attracted to, but try to remember that you need to avoid making the same mistakes you did with all of your previous relationships.

- Equality should be encouraged and respected:

Especially in a new relationship when individuals are still getting to know each other.

However, this equality doesn't mean that you will not be discerning in what's right for you or not. But it does mean that you both will treat each other in the same matter and neither of you will be "worth" more than the other one.

- Your communication will be effective. This can be because you are not trying to guess what the other person is thinking.

Also because you are now aware of how vital efficient communication is to make the other individual understand our points of view, our ways of thinking, and our personality traits.

- Your self-esteem will not be tied up to your partner's mood.

Sometimes we have a terrible day, and everything seems to be complicated. Our car just broke down, our boss has asked us to do more work, and on top of that, your partner is also going through a difficult time with his own life.

Before, when you were highly codependent still, you would have done everything your partner wanted you to do, despite the consequences.

Now you are aware, you will diligently navigate through these small waves, and you will understand that your self-esteem, self-love, and self-worth are non-negotiable.

- Both parties should become aware of specific behaviors and patterns, especially if you would like to move on as a couple.

The need to feel needed is something that you have left behind, and you both should agree on this if you would like your relationship to thrive, to evolve, and to represent what is inside of your heart.

Chapter III: Self-esteem and how we think about ourselves.

You have now learned about codependency. You have become aware of what codependency is, what its symptoms are, and how to overcome the issues that it can bring to your life if you let it happen to you.

In addition, you have understood the importance of having healthy self-esteem, because this will determine whether you will have issues with yourself and others in any particular moment in your life.

Have you ever considered yourself unworthy of something? Perhaps you feel like you don't deserve to have that job you love, or you don't deserve being with the person you have next to you?. Or maybe you feel like you were born with a significant amount of luck and you feel uncomfortable with it, almost like you should have a different life altogether because yours is too good to be true?.

Unfortunately, these feelings are too common nowadays, especially since individuals cannot see their true self-worth. It is like we are always hiding behind a dark curtain, and we think we should stay there; otherwise, we would risk finding out hurtful truths about ourselves.

But, the thing is, we cannot hide from ourselves, and we shouldn't think like we are not worthy of even going deeper within ourselves because we are afraid of what we might find. Your self-esteem will show you clearly everything you must work on, but this will only be the case if you allow yourself to see.

Self-esteem and different cultures

Life had become safe for individuals and people had to focus on how to live life, instead of how to survive life. Therefore, philosophers started to appear, mainly since everybody was asking too many questions and receiving too little answers.

It was Socrates who once said that "everybody should pay more attention to the upkeep of their own souls", and he mentioned this when he was waiting for his execution to take place. Once he finished saying those words, he had already changed the world's history.

Even though this concept of self-esteem is relatively new, the idea behind it is as old as ancient civilizations! If you think about it, it makes sense. If a civilization wanted to survive, they had to take care of themselves (collectively and individually) in order to divert possible dangerous people who would have liked to hurt them.

Of course, self-esteem back then wasn't something clear, it's not like ancient cultures had agreed on protecting the individual's self-worth, but there are hints that something similar to this had happened in many areas of the world.

The level of our love for ourselves can determine many outcomes later on in our lives

For example, did you know that self-esteem is related to academic achievements? So if your self-worth and self-esteem are low, then it's very likely that you will end up getting bad grades at school as well. And the contrary occurs too, if you have watered yourself and you have allowed yourself to grow, then this result will be seen in your final grades.

So, it can be argued that self-esteem is the perception you have about yourself. It will materialize itself in how you love, nurture, value, respect, and care for yourself without the need to have someone behind you to remind you of this. Your self-esteem will become a part of your identity, and it will be a necessity whenever you are trying to understand yourself and others.

When your self-esteem is healthy, you will also have a healthy sense of self-worth and a sense of personal ability because you will also show signs of self-confidence and self-respect. It's all about the self! Because it is at the core of who you are. It's not about what the others think about you (even though this, of course, may also play an essential role in your life), but right now, it's all about you.

During the first couple of years of your life, you will start creating and developing your self-esteem. Your parents or your careers will try to educate you and teach you behaviors that will make each fall in a different category.

In essence, this is socially acceptable; this is dangerous; this may cause you anger; this may be reasonable, and so on. They will also allow you to see for yourself what these behaviors mean to you. Your education will be based on your family's ideal education, and this also means that your path (whether you like it or not) has been established by another person besides you, at least for when you are young.

But this can also cause problems, especially if your views discern your parent's beliefs. So, when do self-esteem problems arise?. If you have low self-esteem you are likely living in fear whenever you get to see yourself again. You may feel like you are rejected all the time or you cannot be satisfied with anything in your life. You distrust everyone else too because you don't trust yourself at all.

You are also very sensitive to what the other person may think of you, and you cannot stop the internal criticism you allow yourself to have regularly. You are often pretending to be someone else, and you could even be giving a false image to the rest of the world because this is one of your defense mechanisms.

You usually depend on others to lighten up your path, and you don't realize that your vision may be all you truly need. And, on the other hand, when you end up receiving feedback from others, you sometimes may feel angry or hurt because they have decided to speak their truth, not yours. You forget you are the one who gets to choose how to live your life, not others.

What happens when your self-esteem is low?

- You are living an unconscious life.
- You are not accepting yourself.
- You are filled with guilt.
- You are not responsible for how you feel.
- You are not authentic.
- You are developing insecurities and fears.

Did you know that your self-esteem depends on you? It is based on how you feel, in your integrity, and in your rationality and way of seeing life.

If you don't have a long look within yourself, then no one else will do it for you. You need to stop for a minute and observe how you are valuing yourself and how you are setting traps for your ego to continue its journey and thrive wherever they get the chance.

Self-esteem is essential because it goes hand in hand with how you take care of yourself. It will also be the driving force for you to achieve your personal goals, aspirations, and dreams.

If you think you have low self-esteem, then try this: think about someone you really love. It could be either a parent, a friend, or even your dog. Then start thinking about everything you love about them. It can be how they make you smile or feel, or it could be a specific trait in their personalities.

Visualize a nice gesture you can do for them and then, under that light, think about yourself, think about how you too are important to others, and lastly, think about a nice gesture you can do to yourself. Enhance your value; this way, you will truly feel it.

Having high self-esteem vs. having low self-esteem

We are not all the same, so it's perfectly normal to have different levels of self-esteem. Some people may have low self-esteem, whereas others may have very high self-esteem. The differences between these two types of individuals may not be sufficiently evident on the outside. However, if you look closely at themselves, you will be able to see their real thoughts and feelings on how they feel internally and how much they think they are worth it.

Some people may be "over-inflated" in regards to how they seem themselves, which is not healthy either. Think about those individuals who often glorify how they look or how great they are at doing something. Of course, there is nothing wrong with doing these, and they shouldn't be ashamed of it, especially if they have worked hard for things. However, once an individual puts himself or herself into a sort of pedestal, then you should be aware of them.

Thus, self-esteem cannot and should not be regarded as a simple statement of high vs. low, because there are many shades of the same word. There must be a balance and parents can teach their children this, but they will first need to work hard on themselves.

Whenever a child says, *"I can't do it,"* or whenever they are expressing frustration, then a parent should be there reinforcing, with love, that he or she can do whatever they set their minds to; therefore, they will succeed. And even if they don't succeed at doing something, they will know how to manage their frustration. This way, they'll see that they can unhook from their negative thoughts and, instead, take an active role in what they want to achieve.

Low self-esteem can also lead to ruminating, which is the tendency to mull over problems, mistakes, or worries, non-stop. Therefore, you made a mistake (or at least you think you did) and then you cannot stop playing the whole situation inside your head repeatedly. You start thinking about everything you would do differently if you had the chance to go back in time, or you start thinking about how it is affecting you and how everything sucks. As a result, you begin withdrawing from the world, because you are too focused on your thoughts.

Childhood experiences are significant in a person's life, as they will contribute to either healthy or unbalanced self-esteem. In other words, when an adult doesn't have balanced self-esteem, it is because, as a child, they were given the necessary tools to develop their self-esteem positively. And sometimes it is quite the contrary, as they were probably reinforced negative thinking patterns or were always criticized.

What about the characteristics of an individual with healthy self-esteem?

Below a small list of characteristics of people with healthy self-esteem:

- They accept the individual differences that we all have because they know each human being has a mind of their own.
- They trust themselves and listen to their inner voice.
- They know they are capable of understanding their values and using them to solve problems that will, no doubt, arise.
- They don't feel guilty if others think differently from them.
- They live in the present moment. They are aware that everything that happened in the past has led them to this right moment.
- They are conscious of their value, and they take care of themselves.

- They are not afraid of failure because they know this will be a future opportunity.

How and where does self-esteem originate, and why is it important?

As stated before, the creation of an individual's self-esteem starts during their childhood and it continues into adulthood. The self-esteem a person has will go through successes, failures, and doubts, and they will work hand in hand with the messages that the individual is continuously receiving from the environment they are in, to translate them and turn them into experiences.

This is why families, teachers, and everybody else who you spend a significant amount of time with is essential. Because they will influence how you behave and how you feel, so, if a person next to you is continuously complaining and being negative, this will affect you. You may end up like them, complaining about everything, or you may be the complete opposite.

However, are there any other reasons why self-esteem is essential? In addition, why should your self-esteem matter to you?

- Self-esteem can either help you or make you fail in some areas of your life.
- Self-esteem can affect the way you think, so your final outlook can be either positive or negative.
- Self-esteem will determine your confidence levels.
- Self-esteem will also affect how you feel about your body.

- Through self-esteem, you will learn how to value yourself and others.

- A healthy self-esteem will make you feel happy and at peace.

- Balanced self-esteem will also show you how important it is to improve yourself.

Why should you teach children about the importance of self-esteem?

Every parent wants to see his or her child grow and develop properly. And for children to achieve this, and become happy, confident, and healthy adults, they must first be happy, confident, and healthy children.

Of course, we are all different, and so are children. Everybody has different needs, issues, problems, and virtues. Nonetheless, having a healthy self-esteem is something we should all look out for because the way you feel about yourself is how you will also perform in your life.

Therefore, children need to feel confident in their abilities to succeed in life. Can you imagine a child who is growing up and he or she is continually being told that they are not good enough or that their efforts are useless? What do you think will happen?. Of course, they will develop negative and low self-esteem, which will lead up to failure in whatever they choose to do.

Think about it this way. Babies and toddlers are remarkably persistent - if you tell them they shouldn't do something, then that's the first thing they will probably do. Babies instinctively know how to do things. They don't need their parents to teach them how to eat, nor how to roll over, sit down, or stand up. They do it because they have practiced enough times to know how it's not done.

What's more, children with healthy self-esteem will thrive at school, are interested and willing to learn from others, can deal with strong emotions, and are able to understand and overcome life's challenges when and if they arise.

How can you help your child's self-esteem?

- Try praising them: whenever they are succeeding or when they are showing genuine effort to do something. If, on the other hand, they have problems when trying to accomplish something, you should also provide some comforting words for them to feel better and try again.

For example, your toddler just learned how to tie his shoelaces, and he's done it by himself for the first time in his life. You should definitely praise him and tell him how proud you are of him.

But what if he wasn't able to do it still? Then talk to him nicely and softly, perhaps you could even teach him a song that will help them to learn how to tie their shoelaces this time around. Either way, make him feel comfortable about the experience of trying to tie his shoelace by himself, instead of focusing on the result.

- Try encouraging them: instead of jumping in every time, they need to do something, try to encourage them to think and act as a way of solving their problems or difficulties.

For example, your daughter always asks for help whenever she wants to go to the bathroom. She says she is scared when you don't help her, so, naturally, you help her all the time and whenever she needs you.

One day she comes to you and asks you to help her go, but right now, it's impossible for you because you are changing your newborn's diaper while you are talking to your partner on the phone. You kindly ask her to go by herself, you encourage her to do this, and you tell her that you will meet her there eventually.

A couple of minutes go by, and she comes back and tells you that she doesn't need your help anymore because she already went and cleaned herself. Why did she do that? Because you kindly encouraged her to do it!.

- Try talking to them about self-esteem: tell them what you think this means and how you work within yourself so you can have healthy self-esteem. Let them know and show them the way to do it as well.

For example, you and your sister are very close in age, so you always ended up doing things together. However, if you two had the same job, she was the one to get fired within the first week.

Your children saw this behavior and started asking questions. *Why is she always like this?*. *"Her self-esteem makes her act this way"*. You would often tell them.

Of course, this is just an example of how you could introduce what self-esteem is. Still, you don't necessarily need this to happen in order to teach your children about what self-esteem is and the importance of having a healthy self-image and self-confidence. You do need, however, to be completely honest with them.

Is what we think of ourselves truly relevant?

Think about it this way: if you think you are a horrible person, then you will not be motivated to improve nor to do anything right. After all, what's the point of even trying if you are already on a low end?. Sounds terrible, doesn't it?.

However, if you have balanced self-esteem, you will see how valued you are to yourself, and you will be motivated to continue on this path. You will peacefully embrace mistakes, and even if you do end up angry sometimes, you will know that this too shall pass.

What you think of yourself will shape your whole world. If you think you are horrible, then the outlook you will have on the other areas of your life will also look gray. On the other hand, if you think of yourself as someone worthy of attention and love, then you will respect yourself and others more.

In addition, you must be aware that your sense of worth shouldn't be related to external factors. So you don't have a balance self*-esteem because your academic success is truly showing now, and you are the best in your class. On the contrary, you are the best in your class because you genuinely care about yourself, and you are motivated enough to be committed to what you are studying.

Lastly...

If you want to do something, then you need to be confident that you will be able to do such a thing. And you can only be convinced if you trust yourself if you know where you stand, and if you have the right tools to develop whatever it is you would like to do.

And once you do this, once you believe in yourself and you are actively going after your goals, you will realize that you also need to fail at some points in order to grow. This acceptance is what life is made of, because, paradoxically, whenever you are finally feeling ready to fail without being attached to the negative aspect of it, you will also understand and come to terms with your imperfection, and you will become more real.

Chapter IV: Strategies for an increased self-esteem

If we want to be comfortable in our skin, and if we're going to enjoy the world we live in, then we must strive for a better version of ourselves.

We need to choose to be happy, where we are building healthy self-esteem, and where we value our journey because it brings us many great lessons.

There are many ways in which we can nurture our habits to have healthy self-esteem, and, luckily for all, we are coming to terms with the importance that self-esteem has in our lives because without this, we would be living in a darker place within ourselves.

These strategies will help you to improve your self-esteem and self-confidence, but you will only be able to achieve these things if you are willing to work hard on yourself. No one else will be able to do this job for you, especially if you consider that you need to remove layers and layers of old habits and past mistakes.

However, you will also be able to use these strategies if you have a child with low self-esteem. And, by doing this, you will even be breaking old traditions and cycles that happen in many generations because they are not aware of the importance of letting go, and also because individuals have not learned yet how to build their self-esteem.

Continue reading and try these strategies out that will help you increase your self-esteem.

1. Understand how your mind works

This is probably the first strategy that will make you open your eyes and see how healthy (or unhealthy!) your self-esteem truly is.

If you are always telling yourself, how awful you are and how you don't deserve anything good, then the chances are that you are stuck in a terrible thinking pattern. You don't know how to release and let go of these negative messages that your inner voice is trying to convince the rest of you.

More often than we would like to admit, our inner critic comes out and starts sending negative and illogical messages that are sometimes too unrealistic and judgmental. And the reason our minds do this is because we let these thoughts go wild.

Have you ever said the following things to yourself?:

"I'm being ignored because he or she doesn't love me".

"I don't deserve to have this family".

"I'm terrible at this, I shouldn't even try it".

"I look awful and pathetic".

"I feel like staying in because I don't get along with anybody. In fact, nobody understands me or how hurt I am".

"I'm hideous, and everybody agrees with this".

"No one will ever love me".

"If I die, nobody will ever notice".

They are pretty harsh and horrible thoughts, aren't they? Not only these thoughts are damaging your self-esteem and mental health, but they are also showing you the dysfunctional areas where you must bring your attention to work on them.

There's no need to spend years of your life ruminating and contemplating these thoughts because they don't bring anything positive in your life. And that reason enough is an excellent reason to stop thinking like that.

But what can you do instead?. Try to tell yourself some positive things. Look at yourself in the mirror and say the following things:

"He or she is not replying to me. Maybe I should ask if everything's okay".

"I deserve to have this family".

"I'm terrible at this, but I will try my best".

"I look great and happy".

"I feel like staying in because I simply feel like staying in today".

"I'm gorgeous, and I agree with this".

"I will always love me".

"I still need to do many things in this life".

I'm not trying to diminish mental health; I know for a fact that it is vital to have a healthy mind because it will lead you to live a healthy life. However, if you start telling yourself every single day that you are happy, eventually you will be happy, or you will think you are happy. Your choice!.

We always hear people say *"you need to take responsibility for your actions"*, well, let me tell you something shocking, you first need to take responsibility for how you talk to yourself. And, if necessary, you will need to recondition your thoughts in order to convert them into positive thinking.

This way, you will start your healing journey, where you will also recover your self-esteem. And this is a much-needed trip you need to make within and with yourself.

Being mindful and practicing mindfulness

These are also excellent choices when you are thinking about having healthier self-esteem. You need to become aware of your unhealthy thinking patterns and habits, and the only way to do this is when you distance yourself from them and start seeing them as they are: thoughts.

You need to become aware of the trap you are setting for yourself, so don't believe everything you think, and don't feel everything you think because your thoughts are only that, words that come and go.

Once you become aware of the thoughts and or troubling situations, you will also start paying attention to how you react to them and how your inner chat is 24/7.

Eventually, what you will want to achieve is very straightforward, although it will probably take you time to get used to it:

- you will need to see things as they are, regardless of whether you think they are good or bad.
- You will need to filter your thoughts, so your mind doesn't become a "thought garbage".

- You will need to convert negatives into positives, and, what's more, you will need to believe them.
- You will need to learn how to differentiate the facts from fiction.
- You will need to stop the constant and negative self-talk.

2. Be transparent and honest with yourself

One of the strategies for increasing your self-esteem is to be willing to explore yourself. This doesn't mean that you need to know about what your strengths and weaknesses are, but you also need to open up your eyes to see new opportunities, feelings, thoughts, and what you can offer to the world.

You also need to be able to adjust your self-image as you grow up. Many people like to live in the old days, where perhaps their life was simpler or where they felt most comfortable.

This is why your self-esteem must go hand in hand with how you feel right now and where you are at the moment. If your self-esteem is an image of an older version of yourself, then this is all based on false imagery of how you used to be.

You are unique!

Did you know it? Did you ever think about how unique you are? Because even though you could share a lot of hobbies or ways of thinking and reasoning with other people, no one else in the world is going to be like you.

And if you would like to honor this uniqueness, then you should stop any comparisons you make regarding yourself and others. Not only are you hurting yourself when you do this, but you are also putting the other person in an uncomfortable position even if they are not aware of it.

You may not even know how to live your life without comparing yourself to others, and this behavior can become very unhealthy, as this will - undoubtedly - have an impact on how you perceive yourself.

It is hard to stop the whole comparison thing, especially when we are so used to doing it, even if we don't mean anything negative. However, you should know that the only person who knows you well is yourself. And this means that the only person you can compete against is yourself. You are unique!

Be practical about how you feel

You have been feeling really lost lately as if you don't know why you are working and doing that job anymore, you seem to feel like you don't fit it like you are not good enough, and you sometimes even question your abilities or the rewards you receive for what you do.

Then one day when your boss is having a terrible day he starts shouting at everyone, especially you, and that's it, that's all it took for you to doubt again about why you are there in the first place. You start reminiscing about how you felt happy during the first couple of years you were working there, but now everything is different, and you feel like crap. You cannot wait to get out of there.

I get it, I have been there as well. You are having difficulties in life, especially in your job, and you cannot seem to come to terms with how you are feeling. Is it just a phase? Or is this the new reality? Should you continue? Or should you reevaluate your life again?. If so, how do you start?.

And you can only start when you are being practical about how and why you are feeling a certain way. But, what does that even mean? It means that instead of feeling vulnerable or sorry for yourself, you will objectively look at your feelings.

Therefore, next time you are feeling like this, grab a piece of paper and a pen, and start writing a list where you will place the pos and the cons of the situation. You could also write or do whatever you feel comfortable with, so if strengths and weaknesses work better for you, then so be it.

The idea behind this exercise is for you to see how your thoughts may be wandering. It will also allow you to put your feelings into words. And, lastly, you will take a weight off of your shoulders because you have expressed yourself.

3. Practice self-compassion

This next strategy is crucial if you would like to increase your self-esteem. By doing this, you will let go of your inner critic and criticism (you know, the one that works 24/7 if you let them), and you will feel a lot more at ease because you will be practicing self-compassion.

I know sometimes it's hard to do it, it's hard being kind to ourselves. We think we don't deserve so many things, or if we do believe we deserve them, we still don't allow ourselves to let go and enjoy them thoroughly.

It's almost as if we need to feel like we have abandoned ourselves in order to thrive because we prefer to feel this way instead of facing the challenges that we are continually attracting into our lives.

However, you should nurture yourself, even if this is something you think you don't deserve. You should be interested in feeding your soul, your mind, and your body in the most conscious way you can, and only you will know how to do it in a way that makes you feel special.

It's not to say that you need to find a grand and spectacular way of showing yourself how much you love and appreciate yourself (although, of course, you could), but you can still have a pure comfort that will make you feel right in the life you are living and that. That coffee you always have in the morning is a blessing, and so is your favorite song on the radio!.

You can have a self-compassion journal where you write about those (and only those) positive feelings, characteristics, impulses, and habits that you have dear to your heart that make you feel good.

Think about how you can continue doing those and ask yourself if you would like to keep them or if you have any other ways to improve them, if necessary. Writing positively will lead you to feel positive about what you are doing.

And this doesn't mean you are escaping reality, quite the contrary, because in strategy number 2 you had to discuss the positive aspects and the negative aspects of a situation, habit, feeling or yourself.

With this strategy, you will discover more positive things about yourself, and it could also lead you to unleash some other passions that were probably dormant. Remember that sewing activity you did a couple of years ago, how much you enjoyed doing it, and how you think about it all the time? Well, now it's your turn and time to materialize your creative spirit.

By practicing self-compassion, you are also managing your goals, and you are in constant awareness whenever you are doing something because your progress is always being tracked. You are presenting yourself with the realities of doing things differently, and this time around, you feel more content and at peace with yourself too, which is excellent for self-compassion.

You could also practice being self-compassionate when you are thinking about past mistakes that have, one way or another, shaped your life. So, instead of revising them with anger or fear, you could be self-compassionate and understand that those same mistakes or errors have now taken you to where you are in this precise moment.

And these mistakes are also present to show you your real colors and who you are: a soul who is trying to find the path in this journey.

4. Visualize constantly

When you visualize, you are taking a couple of minutes to see yourself under a different light. It means that you should invest a couple of moments each day thinking about how you would like your life to turn out.

For example, are you thinking about going into med school? Visualize yourself wearing the mandatory uniform, see yourself going into your school, think of yourself as someone who is already studying the subjects. This way, you will set the path for your needs and desires, and you can make a huge difference by doing this.

Some individuals have problems whenever they try to visualize themselves doing something. Some may feel silly, while others may feel like they simply cannot think about the future because they are too focused on their right now.

If you are one of these individuals, then I'll just give you a couple of tips that will help you visualize in any shape or form:

- You don't have to visualize for your future down the line. In fact, you can start imagining your immediate future; for example, each morning, you can sit down and visualize how your day will be. Think about everything you need to do and how you are going to get it done. Think about how good it is that you can take these couple of minutes for yourself.

- These things you are visualizing doesn't have to be big things that could take you months to get used to or even years. For instance, you can imagine yourself not getting angry today with your toddler because he didn't want to eat his food. Instead, you could think about how you can offer food to your toddler without him saying no.

- If visualizing and sitting down is not your thing, then you can always get moving and imagining when you are active. These short breaks or changes in the routine will definitely help you.

- Visualize it but make it pretty: sounds funny, doesn't it? But we always think that visualizing can only be done inside our minds, and we cannot materialize our thoughts and turn them into art. And this is wrong! You can imagine yourself and express yourself through an art form of your choice. Are you good at drawing? Then draw how your vision is. Are you good at photographing? Then photograph how your vision looks.

Do the right thing for you

This could mean that your vision is sometimes blurry, and you start following another person's idea instead of yours. The important thing here is that you need to follow your dreams if you would like to have a good life, and you need to really live up to this.

So if your visualizing takes you to want to get up each day at 6 a.m, then start visualizing yourself doing so. Or if you would like to go out jogging at nights, then so be it, because those things are your impulse and they are a representation of what's making you happy.

Visualizing is relatively easy. Now comes the active part of the plan!

5. Try something new

It's not always easy to let go of our own judgments and internal criticism, especially when we decide to try something new for the first time. But it is gratifying once we get ourselves over, and we overcome our anxiety, and we finally have the power to try something different, something we have never done before.

Here are some of the things that you could try, especially if you are looking into ways of increasing your self-esteem:

- Try to meditate: there are thousands of benefits directly associated with meditation. Once you start developing a regular practice, you will also conclude that your life seems more straightforward, your breathing techniques have become better, and you now feel more focused than ever before. When you meditate, you are regaining your self, whereas your body is receiving a much-needed rest.

- Learn something new: where you will test your abilities and where you will acquire many more ways to materialize your inner feelings. It could be anything, from learning a new language to taking a course that's completely different from your career path; the choices are endless!.

- Get out of your comfort zone: perhaps you have always been scared of going out on your own or traveling on your own, then this is precisely the sort of feeling that won't let you evolve. Think about it without holding any judgments, though, and see if you could challenge yourself to think and eventually go outside of your comfort zone. So, perhaps next time you go on holiday abroad, you could do it by yourself instead of always waiting for somebody else to become available to go with you.

Motivate yourself throughout the day

So, you started thinking about going for a run, because it's something that you have never done before? Great news! However, precisely this week, a storm has been approaching your town, and the weather is horrible.

You will have to postpone going for that first run because you can't risk your life or your health for a habit you decided to take on earlier in the month.

Or, you could stop that inner chat and make yourself more resilient and useful. So, that weaker voice that tells you "it's okay to stay in, just put a movie on and order a take-away", needs to be led towards "okay, I can't go out for a run, but perhaps I can do a different type of exercise inside of my home".

Do you see the difference there? Your thinking patterns and how you motivate yourself will not only say a lot about you but will also lead you into action.

Remind yourself of the positive side, always!

If you are looking into a significant way of motivating yourself on that healthy and healing journey, where your self-esteem to become more balanced, then you should shift your perception.

This way, you will be reminding yourself of all the positive thoughts, emotions, actions, and benefits that you are constantly receiving by shifting your perception of yourself.

Your goals will become exciting without attaching too many negative thoughts onto them, you will have more energy throughout the day, and you will help yourself to navigate through difficult times, if necessary.

Once your list is done and you have already accomplished some of the goals you set yourself, then you can place it somewhere that's visible for you to have a constant reminder that you did it; you actually did it!.

6. Don't procrastinate

We all know that procrastinating is so attractive, especially when we are doing things that we don't want to or are obligated to do. Procrastinating makes us believe that we are putting some things on hold because we can when in reality, we are putting them on hold because we don't have enough strength to do those things.

However, if you would like to change your mind and how you continue to react towards things, you will soon realize that you need to stop and change patterns and habits that are not necessarily healthy and that you have acquired and made your own.

And procrastination is one of them. So, what can you do? You could change your procrastination and become actively organized instead. You can rearrange your life so that you can effectively do the things that need to be done first. You need to learn how to prioritize opportunities, thoughts, and ideas.

You need to have discipline if you want to succeed, but this won't come to you quickly as you will need to overcome many thinking patterns that you have accepted.

Life goes on

There are many times when you will start questioning everything in your life. From the choices you made for yourself to the options you created with others, everything will seem like it's unreal at some points. And this is normal because, as human beings, we are also thinking people, therefore our thoughts are constantly changing as well, just like we are.

We want to know more about our essence and how this affects or not our self-esteem. We become more curious about our attributes, our personalities, and our particularities, whether they are harmful or not. But once we become aware of them, we can go two ways: we could start swimming in a sea of self-knowledge where we are looking for improvement, or we could easily fall into the procrastination pattern once again and forget about our journey.

The important thing for you to notice is that you can choose the path that will benefit the most to you, and this will automatically take you onto a road of happiness that will significantly increase your self-esteem. If you are conscious of who you are and you are aware of this consciousness as well, then you are halfway there.

As humans, we have a much larger brain that has evolved in comparison to animals. This part of our bodies has been designed this way so that we can learn to control ourselves. Otherwise, we could live with many destructive impulses, and we will be looking for ways into channeling them as if they were urgent and necessary impulses, which they are probably not.

Thanks to this consciousness, we can choose between what we think is right and what we believe is wrong. We also have a free will that allows us to develop plans in which we place all our hopes, in order to achieve objectives with which we identify and feel comfortable with, and, what's more, we are able to choose how to spend or invest our time.

If you are continually procrastinating, you are wasting your time and energy, and you are not getting anything in return. And, on the other hand, you are not effectively working on yourself, which could possibly mean your self-esteem will start to deteriorate again because you are not finding positive ways to help it.

7. Clean everything

Did you know that cleaning and organizing things are therapeutic? Because whenever you are cleaning your house, you are cleaning your soul, and whenever you are cleaning your life, you are cleansing your thoughts as well.

If you would like to become more organized than what you have been thus far, then you could start making lists of things you need to get done. These lists will help you to become more productive, but, at the same time, you will learn how to prioritize what you have to do without procrastinating too much.

Here are some useful tips to become more organized:

- Write down specific tasks that need to get done. Once you start detailing them, you could also write a line or two on what -specifically- needs to be done and how to do it. This way, you'll start sketching a plan.

- You could divide the tasks you have to do. For instance, split them up by their size; this way, you'll see more clearly what you need to do first and what you need to leave to the last item of your list. Cleaning a house is not the same as building a website, hey!.

- If, on the other hand, the task is too large to do in one go, then you will probably have to split it into one, two, or many more parts in order to complete it. This could take hours, days, months, or even years. But you know you will achieve it because you are allowing yourself to follow short and straightforward steps instead of looking at the more significant task in disbelief because you don't know how to tackle it.

- Don't hesitate to be harsh with your tasks! Eliminate them, cross them, put them in the trash once you complete them. Sometimes you will also realize that you cannot do something. Some other times you will think you don't want to do this other thing. And it's all good, you cannot and should not make it all. This is why writing your tasks is good, and why prioritizing is even better because you will see what is working for you and what's not.

- Talk to yourself about the short, medium, and long term and the goals you have in mind. This way, you will avoid feeling overwhelmed by your list of goals.

- Start today! Many individuals leave everything to the last minute. I'll clean the house when it gets filthy, I'll declutter my wardrobe for the new year next month. I'll cleanse myself in six months when I feel ready for it. And so on. What they don't see is that they are leaving everything to the last minute, but what if that minute never comes up?.

- Take advantage of the moments you have right now, start perceiving them correctly and enjoy them. Your organization will depend on how you look at yourself; therefore, if you are organized or not will also depend on your self-esteem.

Cleaning also means forgiveness

You cannot have a clear mind if your heart is filled with anger, disappointment, frustration, and negative thinking. So you have to forgive yourself and others if you truly want to live a healthy life.

Forgive yourself and ask others to forgive you, too, even if it's done in a ritual or a symbolic way. This way, you will feel like a weight has been taken off from your shoulders, and you will be more compassionate and sympathetic towards yourself and others.

Forgive, understand and move forward

Those words should be your mantra from now on because they will be absolutely necessary on this path you are traveling. At some point, you may feel it's not right to forgive someone else or yourself because those same old negative thoughts are invading you again. However, you should really be aware that your mind can be playing tricks, and you could also be led to sabotaging yourself, which is never good either.

What about if you are afraid of failure? How can you overcome those feelings without compromising your need to feel encouraged to do things? Well, you will need to become aware that your failure is only temporary, especially if you don't truly see it as an ultimate defeat. On the contrary, failure will become a permanent failure if you give up and do nothing about it to help you reverse the situation, and if you let it win.

That is when you must forgive yourself and thus continue forward without forgetting your mistakes since these are some teachings that you decided to learn at the time. Nothing will ever happen in your life unless you accept it in the beginning.

The best of it? It is that you are going to learn so much about yourself that you will begin to travel a path of empathy towards others. This will also help you forgive people or situations from your past that may still be affecting you. Are you ready to clean yet?.

8. Learn to communicate effectively

The path of life and your way in your healing journey will also bring awkward moments daily; there's no doubt about it. But you cannot just focus on them. Otherwise, your life will become a tedious process where you won't even enjoy your evolution.

There's no point in following all of these strategies if your mind still wanders in dark thoughts. There's no point in overcoming your codependency and having healthier self-esteem than before if you are still an unhappy person who doesn't really know what they want.

You have to talk to yourself nicely, as silly as it sounds. You already know that the way you speak to yourself says not only a lot about you but also about your habits and your self-esteem, so look at yourself in the mirror and give yourself some love!.

If you scold yourself all the time, then it is unlikely that you are a happy, calm person, with a high enough self-esteem so that you can cope consistently and peacefully through life.

It is because of this that you must find the best way in which to express yourself and speak positively, but, knowing that it is necessary to call attention to specific points from time to time.

Ask for help when needed

And don't be afraid to reach out to others, especially during difficult times. People with low self-esteem tend to keep quiet whenever they are dealing with problems or issues that take over their minds; sometimes, they are afraid that no one else will understand them; other times, they feel ashamed to have to go through that situation.

You need to ask for help if you need it and, likewise, you need to offer your advice whenever another person needs it. You could ask those you trust for help, or you can go to a therapist or a psychologist (or any other related professional) if you don't have anyone to talk to and express yourself. This way, you will hear other perspectives, opinions, and choices that could make you see your problems under a different, lighter note.

Chapter V: Jealousy: why do we feel it?

Jealousy is maybe one of the most human emotion, and it can have a huge impact on our life due to all the unhealthy decisions it can lead to. Everyone on this earth has experienced jealousy at some point in his or her life.

From being upset about your partner's past to being jealous of your friend's job or even being jealous of your ex-partner's new wife or husband, jealousy can take many different forms. However, they all have one thing in common: a healthy emotion turns into an unhealthy and irrational feeling.

If you are in a relationship, you or your partner could become jealous in no time, and, if you let it run over your lives, then excessive jealousy can also present itself and even destroy your relationship.

But can this feeling be looked over? Can you make a relationship work despite being jealous? Is the threat behind jealousy something real? Or is it all in our minds?. The truth is that jealousy can quickly become a scary feeling that will undoubtedly make you feel overwhelmed. In addition, it could even lead to other more serious problems, such as stalking, physical or emotional abuse, or even death in the worst-case scenario!.

You shouldn't think that jealousy will disappear with time or that you or your partner will feel better once you spend 24/7 together. Quite the contrary, if you don't work on your jealousy, then it will go deep-rooted within yourself, and it will start branching out into so many more problems that you won't even be expecting.

This is why it takes a real effort and awareness on your behalf to overcome your jealousy feelings. However, it is not impossible to move on from them, to let them go, and to finally find peace within yourself and within your relationship.

To some people, jealousy means they may lose everything

Some people may not be jealous before they are in a relationship, and all of a sudden, they start feeling like they are about to lose that special bond they have hoped for so long. They have an aversion to anything regarding their relationship, but more so once they start thinking that their partner has a choice as well, and he or she could end things whenever they feel like it.

If you think about it, jealousy is more familiar with individuals who are in a romantic relationship, in comparison to any other type of relationship. People don't usually get jealous if a best friend also has other best friends. Or if your mom has another child, and so on. However, once individuals form a loving and romantic relationship, then everything seems to change, it's like the other person is somehow part of your property. You need to feel secure and safe with him or her.

Do we learn to become jealous, or are we born with jealousy?

Jealousy can start at a young age, and I genuinely believe that it is a learned evolutionary behavior that reflects a lack of self-confidence of the individual who suffers from it. A baby feels abandoned when his or her parents don't pay attention to them, and, if they have a sibling, they may also feel rejected and in need to survive. Thus they become jealous of the other person and will try to catch the parent's attention.

Even though jealousy could be seen as a natural emotion, it can also be argued that jealousy is a behavior that an individual has seen in a different person and is now trying to copy it.

In addition, different cultures may be prone to follow certain cultural norms that encourage behaviors such as jealousy, anger, and even envy.

That's why many people decide to get married in the first place, for example. Not because they love each other, but because they are following specific social, economic, and cultural rules that have been imposed for many hundreds (and even thousands) of years ago, and people are still expected to follow these rules.

Different types of jealousy

Some people don't know that there are several types of jealousy. For example, a person can have normal jealousy, unhealthy jealousy, or retroactive jealousy. Here is a short explanation of each one of them:

Normal jealousy

It's when you occasionally feel jealous, but you realize about this feeling you are having. You brush it off because you know it's an irrational feeling that could damage your relationship, especially if you let it grow and become something entirely negative.

A normal relationship could make you think that you shouldn't take your partner for granted and that you should also consider each day at a time. It could also make you feel motivated to start working on yourself and to appreciate your partner even more.

If you ever have a feeling of jealousy in the normal phase, then you will also understand how it is sometimes essential to feel this way, as it will make you rethink about how your life and your relationship is going.

Unhealthy jealousy

This type of jealousy is very irrational, intense, weird, it usually dominates your way of thinking and acting, and you will feel like you can snap and become violent or abusive in no time.

Unhealthy jealousy also means that you are so overwhelmed by your emotions that you cannot think straight, and as a result, you are trying to control what your partner feels, thinks, does, or says.

Lastly, when you have a feeling of unhealthy jealousy, you will not trust anyone but yourself. And even this trust is something fake, as you will doubt everything. If you truly believed in yourself, then you wouldn't be thinking about your partner leaving you, you wouldn't be trying to guess what the future may hold, and you wouldn't feel anxious about your relationships.

Retroactive jealousy

When a person suffers from retroactive jealousy, it means that they are feeling anxious, jealous, angry, and upset about their partner's old love life.

They will start thinking about who his or her partner used to date in the past, how they would behave with their other halves, and how their relationship was.

On top of this, they would also be constantly comparing themselves to their exes, and it can all become too intense, especially if the partner knows about what's going on in the mind of the jealous person.

What are the signs of an unhealthy jealous person?

It's not difficult to identify a person who suffers from jealousy. For example, when a person is feeling *"normal jealousy"*, they would probably discuss their feelings alongside their partner, and they would let them know how uncomfortable they may be with what's going on. They will also find common ground in the whole situation. They will likely move forward with no more problems whatsoever, because they are both committed individuals and because they are both secure about how they feel.

On the other hand, people who have unhealthy jealousy problems usually bring some other issues to the table. For example, they are always worried about not being loved enough or that nobody understands them, or they are excessively questioning their partner's abilities, decisions, and behaviors.

They want to know everything about their partner, from where they have been to how long they spend with other individuals. A person like this could even start reading their partner's email or phone, "just out of curiosity," and hoping to find something that will incriminate the other person.

An unhealthy jealous person always responds to insecurities and fears, and they may even have severe mental problems when trying to decipher what their partner is doing, how they are feeling, and why they are doing some things.

What causes a person to be jealous?

Usually, people who feel jealous of others have untreated fears that they have carried around for a long time. They may feel anger, grief, pain, self-pity, their self-esteem may be at an all-time low, and they tend to struggle with their partner because they don't trust them enough.

In addition, jealousy can arise if you start feeling like this:

- You have unrealistic expectations of the relationship you are in and of the partner you have chosen. For example, you may have moved in together too quickly because you thought the other person was "the one" and now you realize the truth behind them. Or you may have been misguided by the feelings of the other person. Either way, you are now finding it hard to understand what's going on in your relationship.

- You are reliving hurtful feelings that you once had. It could be that either of your parents moved away from your family home or that a close family member died and you felt abandoned by them. Perhaps you were too little when this happened, and you didn't know how to overcome this issue.

- You don't realize how much you are worth and how insecure you have become. This could be the biggest problem, especially if you are reluctant to open your eyes.

- You are constantly worrying about being alone because you don't know how to be by yourself and with yourself.

- You must be in control at all times, and it's unpleasant when things don't go your way.

What are the consequences of being a jealous person?

As always, the way you react towards something could either have a positive or negative consequence. Couples tend to misinterpret jealousy, and they think it's love instead of a lack of confidence. And, if left untreated, this could become a severe issue that could last for a very long time.

But what are the consequences of being jealous?

- You are always feeling resentful, and you are defensive about things. You and your partner are not even able to talk about how you both feel because you are likely going to explode any minute now.

- You don't trust yourself or others. Thus, how can you be in a relationship if you are always thinking the worst about the other person?.

- You have intense emotional reactions that could hurt others. You are not afraid to become violent if you need to express yourself this way. It may also seem like you don't know how to channel your feelings, and these emotions can turn into physical symptoms as well.

What are some characteristics of individuals who don't experience jealousy?

- They have healthy self-esteem.
- They are self-confident and are aware of this.
- They do not define themselves as a jealous person because they know about the hidden connotations this may have.
- They are not interested in making their partner feel like a possession.
- They are not threatened by how their partner feels or thinks.
- They are very comfortable with who they are and what they have become. They are also very satisfied with the relationship they have.

Lastly, people who know about the dangers of being jealous understand that jealousy can make you act terribly; thus, it could even take you as a hostage without you knowing. You can do many things if you want to overcome your jealousy, but you must be willing to do those things and correct some of your old thinking patterns if you're going to let go of these feelings.

Differences between envy and jealousy

Sometimes people get confused thinking about jealousy and envy because they seem so similar. However, the two of them are different in some other aspects. When you are experiencing envy, you usually see somebody, and you wish you had what they have, or you want you to be like them. It's like your body starts tingling all of a sudden because you like what you see on the other person.

What's more, this tingling sensation doesn't necessarily mean you will feel jealous of the person, you just wish you had what they had, and that's it. In other words, you can be envious of somebody or something else, but you also like what you see, so you have something in common with them.

For example, one of your friends is looking better than ever before! You go towards her and ask her what her secret is and how did she get in shape. She tells you she started this new fitness regime five times a week, and she loves it! You then ask her to give you more details because you are interested in changing your lifestyle as well. You don't tell her, *"I have envy, and I would love to be like you"*, but you do say *"you look great and I'm looking forward to looking great as well!"*.

This type of envy will make you feel motivated about yourself, and you will probably end up getting in great shape because of what a friend told you, but most importantly because you liked what you saw.

However, using the same example, let's say you saw your friend who is now fitter than ever before. She got this new body thanks to her diligent hard work at the gym and because she started eating healthily. She told you about this, and you heard everything she had to say, and you still went around telling all of your friends that *"she got her body like that because she had surgery"*.

Not only are you lying about it, but the fact that you can't have what she has (because you are not working hard and you are not eating healthily), you are also spreading rumors about someone else just to damage their reputation. This is why jealousy can be destructive if you let it consume you, especially when you are in a state of mind where you think you can control another person's life and the narrative behind them.

It's normal to feel jealousy at some point or another, especially when you are finally waking up to how you are living your life and when you intend to become more conscious about yourself and your surroundings.

However, sometimes we jump from feeling a little jealousy here and there to go on a jealousy rollercoaster where we cannot seem to stop because we are addicted to its speed. We start getting consumed by our feelings, and we forget that we are here because we need to learn from our lessons, and we only have this life to be lived, so what are you going to do? Are you going to waste your precious mornings thinking about things you don't have, and others do?.

Or are you going to invest your days visualizing correctly and in a positive light and thinking and materializing everything you would like to accomplish? It's definitely up to you how you get on with life. Still, listening to this audio book means you are on the right path as you found a guidance that will lead you to the light that's always on at the end of the tunnel.

Chapter VI: How to manage jealousy in relationships

Some people think that jealousy is a sign of love and that whenever they have this feeling, then they are usually trying to express how much they care about the other person. But, in reality, this isn't the case, and we may even be trying to hide the truth from ourselves.

Jealousy can bring the worst of you, especially if you know that there isn't a distinction between "good" jealousy or "bad" jealousy. It's all the same: jealousy. So, don't try to pretend that if you feel a "little bit" of it is because you are genuinely caring about your partner.

However, you may be wondering, if jealousy is a real feeling, then how can you overcome jealousy in your relationships? Is it possible? Or should you just accept the fact that you will feel jealous of your partner for the rest of your relationship?.

Here are some common strategies you could implement in your life in order to overcome jealousy in your relationships:

    1. Understand your emotions:

Close your eyes and feel yourself. Imagine you are with another person, and you become a toxic individual who is always jealous of the other one. And do not forget that jealousy starts with something small; sometimes, you may not even realize once you start becoming jealous.

Then it can blow up without you thinking, and you will still not even look behind and say, *"how did I even get here?"*. And that's a real problem because you are not being aware of how you have been acting and, therefore, you do not understand how your emotions are working.

But understanding your emotions should go further than this: what is exactly the thing that makes you jealous about your partner?. Is it seeing them talking to other people?. When you hear them talking to their ex?. When they go out without you?.

Then you should try this exercise:

- Visualize yourself doing the thing you are jealous of whenever your partner does it. So, if you get jealous when your partner talks about his or her ex, then you will visualize yourself talking to your new partner about your ex. Do it naturally, because you don't have anything to lose. Say everything you have ever wanted to share. Now visualize your partner doing exactly the same thing. But this time, you won't feel jealous about it because you are now able to detach yourself from the situation, just like your partner did when you were talking about your ex.

Being jealous means you are having problems with your self-love, not that you are having issues with the love you are sharing with the other person.

2. Be emotionally independent

This point goes hand in hand with point 1. Frequently jealousy is caused by your fears, insecurities, and your need to become possessive of things and feelings. These emotions distract you from pure love, and they will contaminate yourself and your relationships.

In addition, jealousy can also turn you apart from your freedom because you will always be and feel the need to be attached to another person, instead of being happy with yourself. On the other hand, jealousy should be looked at as an indication of the things you need to work the most, and you must treat it maturely as it could show you the way to re-establish and strengthen your relationship with yourself and others.

Once you become emotionally independent, you will know how to overcome your jealousy, but you cannot become independent and still be jealous of your partner. But how can you reach this?. You should first answer the following questions:

- You first need to see what triggers this emotional response of jealousy. Are you reliving fears you had as a child?. Is your new relationship bringing you memories of an old relationship or problems you had when you were younger?.

- How do you feel when you are jealous? Does it feel like you become a different person?.

- Are you happy when you are jealous? Does it feel like a "safe place" to be in and live in that state of mind?.

Becoming emotionally independent will require a lot of work on your behalf, especially if you see it as a goal for the rest of your life, so you will stay in that state-of-mind instead of going back to it whenever you feel distressed or jealous.

3. Embrace your individuality

It is very common to want to spend as much time as possible with your partner, especially if you are entering a new relationship. Every minute of each day doesn't seem long enough when you are with someone you genuinely love.

This time spent together is often idealized as something romantic and passionate, especially because you may feel incomplete if you are not together. However, this could also lead to jealousy if, and when, you both decide to start doing things separately. In fact, it could lead to anxiety as well because you will start questioning the other person's motives and activities.

As a result, your individuality and your time will be compromised because you are with someone else, and this shouldn't be the case. On top of this, spending too much time together at the beginning of any relationship could be unhealthy, especially when things are being said that could be very ambiguous, and they are, in fact, an obvious sign of jealousy.

So, if your partner is saying or has said these things to you, then you should be questioning them:

- "Nobody else will ever love you as I do".
- "I am the perfect person for you".
- "I can't bear the thought of sharing you with another person".
- "I could be with your forever".
- "You will never find another man or woman like me".

Of course, these statements don't necessarily mean that your partner is controlled by his or her jealousy, but it should serve as a warning that perhaps there is more to see about this person than you previously thought.

Pay attention to the conversations you have, and always trust your instincts. And it may be a horrible thought, but be prepared to lose the other person, especially if your self-esteem is going downhill because of them. Nobody will ever be worth your healing time and opportunities! You must place yourself first all the time. And this is not ego, it's called self-love, and you should definitely practice it.

4. Stop comparing yourself to others:

Even though it is not easy, you should stop comparing yourself to others, and you should definitely stop minimizing yourself and your achievements just because it may seem other people have better life.

Most individuals who suffer from jealousy also have low self-esteem in the background. They don't understand why their partners love them or how they are in a relationship because they don't realize how much they are worth. Thus they start comparing themselves to everybody else, and their happiness solely depends on how they see themselves throughout the eyes and lives of others.

And this is exhausting!. Imagine thinking about others all the time instead of thinking about you?. Someone is always better looking, more prosperous, intelligent, happier, etc., etc., etc. than you. But nobody is LIKE YOU!. And this is a surprising fact to some; you are a unique person in this world, so start acting like one.

5. Believe in the other person

Or, better yet, choose to believe the other person. Not everybody wants to hurt you, even if we live in a world that is sometimes horrible. Learn to trust the people you love, and, quite rightly, be confident in yourself when you choose to distrust over a person.

Jealousy could hurt your relationship if you are snooping around for evidence that your partner is cheating on you, and you don't trust him or her enough. If you do distrust them, talk to them, hear what they have to say and learn from them as well.

Don't try to hide your feelings because you feel guilty about distrusting your partner. It may sound odd, but you should trust your partner unless they have given you reasons not to believe. In that case, always ask yourself if the relationship is worth keeping, and if you are willing to overcome these trust issues in the long run?. If not, then reconsider your relationship, you always need to remember that you should trust your feelings.

On the other hand, it's very tiring to be doubting your partner's word or behavior all the time. This won't lead you anywhere either, but it could lead them to have an affair or any other type of erratic behavior if they don't feel like you trust them at all.

Find the strength within you to believe your partner and to see through them, if you think it's worth it. But do remember, some relationships are worth keeping and maintaining, whereas others are simply in our lives to teach us a valuable lesson so we can move on and only you can make up our mind about this.

6. Stop wanting to have control of everything

One of the earliest signs that should serve as a warning for you in any relationship is once they start trying to control every aspect of your life.

For example, saying the following things can be seen as an alert:

"You shouldn't wear that dress if you are going out".

"I don't think you should go out with that person".

"I'm not happy if you see the mother or your child".

"I would rather if we don't talk about your friends anymore".

If you ever hear those phrases, then you should know your partner is unhealthily jealous of you, and they are trying to control your life and how you handle things, and of course, this isn't acceptable nor fair.

Or, what's worse, perhaps your partner is not saying these things. Still, he or she are checking your phone behind your back, they are sending you emails from fake accounts, or are even demanding to know where you are throughout the day, then you should really consider having a serious chat with them to see what's going on in their mind.

Once you discuss this issue, you may be able to sort it out or to dive in and discover behavior that is more erratic ultimately. Either way, you should become aware of the importance of your privacy, and you should be able to receive some respect, especially if you are also respecting the other person.

At the end of the day, nobody should ever have a say on what you wear, who you hang out with, who your friends are, or any other choices you make throughout life. This does not mean that you will always be right and no one is ever allowed to question you, but there's a big difference between doing this out of love and doing this out of jealousy.

7. Understand that everybody is free to choose

Following the same line of thinking, everybody should come to terms with the fact that everyone is free to choose what they want to be, who they want to be, the things they all like, and how to live their lives.

Also, people can choose whether they are comfortable when being jealous of their partner or whether they are comfortable when being with a suspicious person. Supporting each other's feelings doesn't equal going over each other's opinions, though, so if you ever feel like you are being stepped on to then, you should seriously question the other person and yourself.

To some individuals, jealousy may seem like a natural behavior, and to some others, this feeling may be a sign of distress. It is all very relative; however, you must have a conversation with your partner about this, because the last thing you need is to have someone lashing out every time you call them to say "hey, I am going to be late tonight".

When you are in a committed relationship, then you are expected to be honest and to take responsibility for how you behave. If you approach this with maturity, then your partner, you should also be honest and responsible for how they behave. Things like "it's not my problem you feel this way" or "you shouldn't be jealous because you know I love you" shouldn't be taken lightly, on the contrary, if you both want your relationship to work and to evolve you must definitely share with each other how you truly feel while at the same time you will respect how you are all free to choose how to feel.

8. Talk about your jealousy

Communication is vital in all relationships, and that is a fact. Whether you are communicating verbally, by signs, or with a simple look, without wanting and being able to communicate, then you wouldn't get to know the other person at all. How do you know if they like something if they never say anything?.

Jealousy is an extraordinary feeling that could take the center of the stage in your relationship easily if you don't talk about it with your partner. This explains why individuals who are in relationships where they tend to keep secrets from each other and where they are not comfortable with sharing the whole truth, then they are also the ones who experience more jealousy.

Find out where this insecurity is coming from and share your thoughts with your partner. You could set aside time for a date, or you could do it spontaneously, but you must talk about it. Growing in a relationship also means that sometimes you have to grow separately too, so if you feel like there are things that you could improve on yourself and will definitely help the relationship to be better, then talk to your partner about it, you may be surprised by what they have to say.

A relationship is a commitment between two individuals, so you two should be willing to discuss things, especially when there are situations that could make you feel uncomfortable.

Lastly, if you feel like you have been jealous for no reason, then you could always ask for forgiveness and move on. The other way around applies as well, though. Be open about your jealousy; it's probably the best thing you could do as this may guide you to become stronger than ever before.

9. Never accept abuse

If there's one thing you should never accept in any relationship, it is abuse. Whether it's verbal, physical, psychological, economic, or spiritual abuse, you should always put yourself first, and you should never think that the jealousy that the other person is feeling is either healthy, okay, or acceptable.

If your partner is jealous and he or she is already displaying signs of abuse, then you should definitely think about the future of this relationship. It's easier said than done, I know, but you shouldn't set unrealistic expectations thinking that they will change because they love you.

The reality is, even if it sounds too hard to admit, is that if they are already in a violent cycle with you, then chances are they will continue this violent cycle and will repeat it over and over again.

Being abusive doesn't happen overnight, and you must be aware of this. You should also know that whenever a person starts exerting their control over you, then you should seriously question this behavior as it could lead to other compromising behavior.

You should also seek help whenever you need it. Many support groups have been set up to help those who are in vulnerable situations inside a violent and abusive relationship.

You should also know that it is not your fault if the other person is being abusive towards you or any loved ones, especially if they keep on telling you that this is the case. Trust your instincts; if they tell you to run away or to seek help, then do it!.

Chapter VII: Codependency: how to say "Stop!"

When you are codependent on a person, or you are codependent on a damaging habit, you probably feel like you can't start something unless that individual or that habit is with you at all times. You may feel like everything's difficult without them and it doesn't matter whether you are trying to do something new or not, you just feel like you can't move or be without them.

Without your codependency, you may feel defeated, like you cannot put a little effort on your behalf in order to continue with your life. It is as if you were paralyzed, without looking at anything, without really knowing what to do and.

Therefore, you do not know where or how to start, because you think, what are you going to start, what are you going to do if you do not know how to act because your codependency has affected your whole being?.

Suddenly you find yourself tired of your daily activities, you cannot stand those who surround you, everything you used to enjoy becomes a problem, and you feel excessively emotional at times. You may even feel that you have many emotional changes going on that do not allow you to continue with your life, and, to top it all, your mind does not stop having intense debates with itself. Are you right? Are you addicted to a person? To a substance?

These are all difficult questions to answer, and thanks to all these emotions, you start to feel distracted, without having a plan for being productive and without a clear focus to guide you. You also feel like you are too attached and too reliant on that person, on that cigarette, on that feeling, you are attached to whatever makes you feel alive.

Being codependent could mean you are dependent on another person, on destructive behavior, or even a feeling. You could be codependent on having low self-esteem because your life has been filled with people who didn't show you how much you are worth, and you are yet rediscovering that by yourself.

Codependency can also mean that you are overly attached to your partner and that you don't like or don't know how to be by yourself and with yourself, despite the fact that you could also be in a romantic relationship.

So, how can you stop all codependency habits that you have that will not let you continue with your life? How can you move on from being entirely and unhealthily dependent on another person? And, what's more, how can you regain your self-worth back?.

Continue reading, and you will find out:

But what habits would you want to change?

- Your habit could be to feel unloved by your partner.
- Another habit could be to have a fear of your partner leaving you.
- You made jealousy a habit.

- Your partner's opinions are more important than yours, and this is another habit.
- You like to demand your partner, even if it's an unrealistic expectation. And guess what? This is another habit!.
- You are aware of how you are acting and reacting, but you tell yourself you cannot change because you were born with these habits.
- You pretend things are great because those things are already your habits.
- You have become an extremely irritable person who doesn't get along anymore with his or her partner.

1. Change your mindset

Did you know that your brain is sometimes anatomically speaking, considered as a muscle?. This is because this part of your body is made up of muscle tissue, and it's made of gray and white matter. In other words, your brain has a physical characteristic that resembles any other muscle of your body. And what do you do with muscles if you want to improve their condition?. Well, you train them!.

Therefore, if you would like to take full advantage of your innate abilities and characteristics, you must also train your brain to do the things you want it to do on your behalf, precisely as if it's a muscle that you are exercising.

But, how is this related to you being codependent?. Simple! If you want to stop being codependent on the person you have a relationship with, then you must train your brain (and the rest of you) either to stop being codependent on them or to become independent of them.

And how can you do this? If you want to stop being codependent, you must train your brain to do so. You should live in a state of mind where mindfulness becomes your nature and where you feel comfortable enough by asking yourself uncomfortable questions. Mindfulness is a state of mind that allows you to understand many of your life's issues, if you let it, of course. And the best thing about doing this is that it's completely free as you cannot pay anyone else to do so for you.

2. The only good confirmation is that one that comes from yourself

As a child, you are always wondering and sometimes even asking your parents if what you are doing is good enough or if you are doing a good job. It is very understandable to go through childhood, asking (even if it's done indirectly) those whom you love the most to help you out so you could form your personality.

However, many individuals start to rely excessively much on their parents, siblings, or any other family member, that will help them to shape their thoughts. It seems like they become detached from what they think and feel and become attached to what others think and feel.

As explained in previous chapters, this is probably rooted in a lack of self-worth, low self-esteem, and even abuse in some cases. But how can a person start seeking happiness outside of themselves? How is the validation of what others think more critical to what they believe?.

How can individuals be stuck in the vicious cycle of wanting to be liked and loved when they can't even do those things for themselves?. When are individuals going to stop asking for outside confirmation that tells them they are good enough or not?.

This is a crazy world, especially if we believe that what the others think is more important to what we think. We are human beings because we have evolved to such an extent that one of the most important traits we have, as a species is our ability to think, solve problems, and philosophy about them.

In addition, if this is one of our most significant accomplishments, then how can we outsource it to someone else? To a person who will let us know whether they like our way of reasoning and thinking or not?. It is now time to start thinking about ourselves and to understand that the only confirmation we ever need is the one that comes from our mind and our heart.

One thing is to know yourself and to appreciate it, and another thing is when you write down everything you love about yourself and how grateful you are for your life, everything, and everybody in it. This isn't an egotistical thing to do; quite the contrary, once you start reading your lists, you will soon understand yourself much more.

3. You must want a change in your life

We are so used to doing things the same way that we don't even doubt them anymore. We are also used to some feelings so much, that it's better to keep them just like that, in case we lose our sense of identity if those feelings disappear.

The point is that you are not willing to get out of your way and to discover new things, and then you will do the same thing and get the same results.

This pattern of codependency will only ever go away if you start establishing and nurturing yourself. The relationship you have with yourself will be the most important one. Even if you have children! It sounds hard, doesn't it? However, think about it, how can you be there for your child if you are codependent on another person? How can you teach your kid to be independent and to live a happy life if you are living another person's life? It's impossible.

You need to lead the way; thus, you need to change if you want to materialize change. And would you like to know a great thing? If you are reading this, it's because you are already on your way to change. Don't get discouraged!.

4. It's okay to take a break every once in a while

It may be difficult, but it's not impossible to do so. In fact, this should have been made a mandatory principle for everyone, and because of how the world is going and all of the current affairs, now it's the time where almost everybody is having a well-deserved break. And it is definitely worthwhile!.

Did you know that you could take a break from your relationship? Especially if you are feeling stressed out or you feel like you two are not really connecting anymore?. It is okay to ask for some time apart and recharge some batteries, and no one should ever tell you otherwise.

You are free to ask for this break, in particular, if you feel like ending the relationship is not what you want deep down yourself. A good solution would be to have a break; this way, if both parties agree, you could start mending your relationship and see if it still has the spark to continue lighting or if it's close to dying off.

A break could also mean that you are spending some time apart. Therefore, you are able to see in a more precise way how and why you are codependent on the other person. Taking a break could lead you to see things in a different light, energy, and perspective.

5. You should establish some boundaries

Did you know that a codependency habit could be that you don't establish any boundaries because you are afraid of what the other person may do or think if they dislike the limit you just put on them?.

What's more, did you know that boundaries can be requested from another person, or they could be placed on yourself? Because, let me tell you something, most of us, if not all, need some boundaries at some point or another in our lives.

Setting limits is something we should all do, especially if you are the type of person who is willing to sacrifice yourself because you need to meet another person's needs. There's an invisible line we all have drawn, and we should never cross it.

A personal boundary will help you whenever you feel unsure about a situation and when you start thinking about pleasing the other person instead of pleasing you. By setting limits, you will also be remaining true to yourself because no one else will be accountable for how you behave. If you let someone else cross your invisible line and you didn't like it, then too bad, you made your choice when you let them in.

Setting boundaries does not only mean you get to say "no" as an answer. In fact, you could talk with your partner about many more limits. For example:

- There are sexual boundaries, especially nowadays, when there has been an increase in open relationships, polyamorous relationships, and polygamous relationships.

- There are communication boundaries, which can range from what you call each other (as in what is your nickname for each other), to what words you definitely don't want to use on one another.

- There are space boundaries. Especially if you are not living together but are spending too much time in each other's places. Or if you are already living together but need to maintain your individuality.

- There are economic boundaries where you both share your money, where you partially share your money, or where you don't share your wealth.

- There are commitment boundaries. Which are usually more common when a couple starts getting to know each other.

If your partner is making you feel guilty because you have set your boundary, then you must have a serious chat with them. This is not an argument that requires someone to win and someone to lose. However, this is an argument that requires two grown-ups who are willing to discuss their boundaries consciously.

Conclusion

After listening this audio book, you should now be aware that stopping your codependency habits is not an easy thing to do, and you will probably have to work hard to find and maintain your life back and to recover yourself fully. It is not a fixed process that you get to do in six weeks' time, but it requires time.

It's a fluid process that should take from scratch and like any other personal journey, you will have difficulties, and you will probably end up confused by some of the choices you have made or by the fears, you have developed. It is all part of the plan, and it should be welcomed during this time when you are healing. Remember that we are human beings, so our nature is to evolve as well, and one of the ways in which you can do this is by stepping out of toxic relationships that will damage yourself.

You have now learned the truth about codependency, what the signs of codependency are and how you need to understand and overcome them. I hope that this guide has taught you the importance of self-esteem and our way of thinking; it has shown you some strategies you could implement to increase your self-esteem, it has proven that jealousy is a real feeling and that you need some strategies like the ones explained here.

And in order to achieve this, you will have to remain honest with yourself, and how you have acted throughout your life, you need to be open about your consciousness and self-awareness, and you need to be willing to try something new that has the potential to change your life completely for a better future.

There is no doubt that you may feel frustrated at some point during your journey, and you probably want to leave everything as it is. You would rather complain once again and feel the discomfort of being in a codependent relationship because that is easier to face all of your internal demons.

But just visualize yourself coming into terms with who you really are, see the potential you have within you, embrace change and accept the new you, love the person you are finally becoming, believe in yourself for wanting to change, and create the happiness you deserve.

You should start today, as this will be the best moment to open your eyes and become aware of your reality. Leaving things for later will only perpetuate how bad you feel and how unhappy you are now.

Be assertive with who you want to spend your time with, but also become confident with your own thoughts and how you canalize your feelings. No one else can do this for you. And once you start realizing how your mind works and the profound effect your words have on your overall well-being, you will understand how important it is to have you and to love you as the first person in your life. No one else is more important than you, and you deserve this happiness and love; don't ever doubt it.

However, it is up to you to react accordingly, so which one are you going to choose? Are you going to put yourself down again, or are you going to rise up from these problems? You have got the right answer within you!.

Lastly, being able to recognize your codependency, your jealousy, and your low self-esteem is only the first couple of steps; you will have to take on this journey. If you really would like to change your life then you must be willing to compromise seeing people who may have a negative effect on your life, you may need to stop unhealthy lifestyle habits, and you will need to make a correct balance of how you are using your energy.

Are you always worrying? Are you never happy anymore? Are you always taking care of others? Who is taking care of you, then?

Always listen to yourself, to your body, to your emotions, to your soul. Understand that the other person that cannot lie to you is yourself, so embrace your inner child and give him or her a hug and the opportunity to shine through the chaos you have created in your adult life.

Once you do this and your inner child has healed, then you will become aware of how your relationships will also start changing, evolving, getting better and overcoming all the problems you may face. You will stop being stuck, and you will learn how to turn your problems into lessons that will teach you a lesson.

Each day is an opportunity for you to change your toxic patterns and to become your authentic self. Long ago were the days where you would always blame another person for your problems, now you have rediscovered the tools you have that will help you understand how you have been navigating this sea called life.

Make some changes that you will not regret, and start living the life you truly want and deserve.

www.ingramcontent.com/pod-product-compliance
Lightning Source LLC
Chambersburg PA
CBHW070930080526
44589CB00013B/1461